Breathing Life into Death...

Poems, Songs & Visions

Pushkara Sally Ashford

Platypus Publishing

Breathing Life into Death...
Poems, Songs & Visions

https://singpeacepilgrimage.ning.com/home

Platypus Publishing
ISBN: 978-196825318-9

Library of Congress Control Number: 2025917710

Dedication

To you...

seekers, poets, songcrafters

and vision keepers:

May your pilgrimage be illumined and
guided by great souls whose love and
wisdom resonate within your own heart.

Contents

Preface

"The jig was up," this much I knew, or sensed, at the first signs that I was losing my voice.

Singing had always at the center of my world. The irony of losing my voice while leading workshops entitled, "In Search of a Voice" was only a small measure of the devastating loss of identity I was to experience as time went on.

What began as an imperceptible interruption in my song was diagnosed early on as spasmodic dysphonia. Gradually, my voice troubles moved from a rocky kind of hoarseness to a choked off and broken speech pattern that could become little more than a helpless squeak. These days, I choose between speaking and breathing.

I was in the prime of my life, not yet 40, and one endowed with vocal gifts. Everything in my life up to then had come from my ability to speak and sing. I was not only losing my currency in the world, I'd lost my "art," my best friend, my childhood comforter and most constant companion. For generations, music-making had been the glue that held our family life together and it, too, was coming apart.

At the time, I held five jobs in as many fields; as a wife, mother of three teens, singer and performer, a co-founder and teacher at an alternative school, and masters level college instructor, I had a finger in too many pies. I made a name for myself in the '70's as the designer-coordinator of a newly funded program addressing Family Violence, and subsequently opened a private practice specializing in family therapy.

Up to then, I had no spiritual orientation. So, what does a self-proclaimed "Godless one" do in the face of debilitating loss? In desperation, I prayed, and my silent cry of "Help!" was heard. An immediate shift in consciousness, a profound awakening, like nothing I could contrive or ever imagine, literally turned my life inside out. My mind was blown!

I'd read that the teacher appears when the student is ready. By whatever miracle of fate, I'd been made ready to receive an answer which came in the form of spiritual initiation by a living master and a path that resonated deeply within me. Six months into my deep dive into yoga and meditation led to my first meeting with my guru, the one whose grace I'd received from thousands of miles away.

I'd been overextended and was not well. A year and a half later, my mind occasionally circled on thoughts of death. My departure during a second visit to my teacher brought on an experience that recurred for years, and many times over. I'd said my goodbyes. As I knelt at my seat, I felt a stabbing wound. My heart seemed to be ripped from my chest. I contracted a high fever. It felt like my bones were being ground to dust. I could barely walk. It took hours for me to make it back to my hotel to pack my bags for my return flight home.

While languishing on my bed at home with the late morning sunlight pouring into the room, my consciousness became sharply alerted. Aware, only, of speedily being drawn downward into a dark, spiraling vortex, I called out, "Help!" My mind's eye perceived that word pulsing and moving upward on a kind of gray mass which suddenly became golden-orange. "Baba's helping." My being relaxed.

The universe had disappeared and my distress was in not finding my body anywhere. A thought floated through the ether to call out to my son. I could hear him in the next room, but I knew he could not hear me from wherever "I" was. Concurrent with these bewildering circumstances was the awareness of an all-pervasive Love, a "Presence" that I can only describe as divine...God, the totality of all that Is.

Meanwhile, gazillions of tiny sparks of firelight had appeared on the screen before me. They were bouncing, rhythmically vibrating on the golden-orange field. Some of them began to move together. Diffuse at first, like the dot matrix in an old color newspaper photo, they coalesced and came to rest.

I could feel my hand on the pillow. Then, with the movement of these tiny sparks, I witnessed my lips forming. Again, diffuse and barely recognizable, they coalesced. As soon as I felt them return to this corporeal reality - my face, I called out.

I was breathless, most clearly blessed but still terrified, as I tried to explain what had just transpired to my nineteen-year-old son. His response as he held my hand was, "This sounds like a case for intense mantra repetition."

I was simultaneously relieved to be returned to my body, while feeling a trace of regret for having abandoned the presence of the purest Love I'd ever experienced. Amazing to me was how quickly my physical strength and stamina was restored. I quickly dressed and joined friends at a class and found them laughing, rolling around with delight in my company - a contact high from the state I'd been held within.

From then on, the fear of death as a conclusion or end point to life in the body left me, never to return. It dawned on me that I'd been gifted a body, reconstituted and revitalized, in which to pursue my chosen path.

I'd gained insight into the continuity of consciousness within the juxtaposition of these two experiences: the "awakening" and "near-death," beyond the limitations of the mind and identification with the body.

Even so, the unresolved trauma of a former violent passing would be replayed time and again upon my departure from the safety and protection of the guru's presence and holy home until its power was finally extinguished and I was able to take full responsibility for my life and stand on my own two spiritual feet.

The healing odyssey sparked by the loss of my singing voice had become a pilgrimage of the soul. I left my home in the Northwest in 1984 to tour and serve my teacher. I lived in an ashram in India for the better part of seven years and traveled a zigzag path, criss-crossing the US for another decade. It took me around the world several times, to people and places I would not otherwise have encountered.

But the real work has always been an "inside job."

Urged by my teacher to "find out about the voice," I sought out and incorporated many healing modalities. When I lost my power to communicate orally with the speaking world, I was rendered "invalid," - first, by myself and by others who surely take the gifts of speech and song for granted. As I result, I resorted to self-inquiry, and a mode of contemplative writing.

In a NYC apartment, poems began to emerge as I lay on the floor on my back, my guitar on my belly, trying to make sound. Visions and inner prompting through dreams were leading me to believe that I was not done with music, but how to proceed with no voice? I heard songs I could not sing.

While in India, I whistled a 4-part arrangement of a chant to an ad hoc, international choir. I set a poem to music among the trees in upstate New York, later recorded by my son. In the hopes of sharing songs yet to be written, I prepared music manuscripts for ensembles and choruses while living in a Seattle apartment. Due to the uncertainty of a secure income or a place to call home, opportunities to hear them performed live were few and far between.

Once settled in a "home with a soul" in the Pacific Northwest since 2002, I was able to share some of my original music with the help of willing singers and musicians in the community.

And I experienced God - "the one who is otherwise beyond perception" - within and around me. Set against the backdrop of my first taste of perfection— the elixir of divine love and the grace of the one who reached out to me—I wrote the poems and songs scattered among the collection of the journals I've kept over half a lifetime.

Because I know the stories underneath these poems and songs, the chronicle of my spiritual journey reads like a novel whose chapters I've been living through. I can see that I was never alone in my quest.

Some of the words I chose to represent my life reflect a sense of limitation and lack, an underlying neediness, a feeling of not being quite good enough. Still, there were the practices of meditation, contemplation, seva, *satsang, darshan*, reading scriptural texts, the repetition of God's name—mantra —to say nothing of dreams and visions, and these supported me on the path that opened to me. These practices have held my fickle mind sufficiently together to bring me to a place of repose in remembrance and genuine respect for the one—myself—who made and kept the commitment to carry on, no matter wha

Inspired by a singing dream in 2008, I designed and commissioned the construction of a "gypsy wagon," a tiny home, for SingPeace! Pilgrimage for Peace & Global Harmony, a journey to share my quest for peace within and all around. For over ten years, troubadours have brought a style of singin' 'n mingling, story-telling, puppetry and exuberant outdoor play to communities around the region. Our mission's reach has been extended through the online presence on a social media site where readers of this book are invited to dialogue and share their own stories, songs and poems.
https://singpeacepilgrimage.ning.com/home

Entering my eighty-sixth year, I am experiencing a blissful renewal and reunion. Confirmation came in a dream where I saw and heard my guru shout in celebration: "Sally's back!" I feel my guru was acknowledging that I'm using my time wisely now.

In a recent meditation vision, the sage, Narada—the divine messenger, devotional journalist, and musician who appears throughout India's scriptures came to me. This mere stick of a man dressed from head to toe all in red with a mane of long black hair put his arms around me. I'd heard the message, "It's already written," and his intimate presence prompted me to cull from my journals this collection of poems, songs and visions.

"Breathing Life into Death" is meant as prayerful encouragement to people on the path to carry on and also to be open to hearing, perceiving, and following the guidance that comes from within.

It is an offering from my heart regarding the enormous, eternal gift of guru's grace.

Acknowledgments

My most heartfelt thanks to family and friends who came forward with help in the process of publishing this book of poems songs and visions.

To my son, David Ashford, for his encouragement and professional expertise during the many hours of consultation, inputting text, formatting, cover layout and design.

To my daughter, Wendy Ashford, for her inspired and colorful art work, photography, sense of humor and hearty laughter.

To my friend and editor, Margaret Bendet, for the hours, acute attention and kindness shown in reading, reviewing and editing the text.

To the team of readers and reviewers behind the scenes who provided feedback and editing advice.

To the brilliant company of saints and fellow seekers who have shown their light, prepared and shared the path, many of whom opened their hearts and homes around the world to me when I had no address to retreat to. The list is nearly longer than the number of pages in this book!

And to the lovely singers and musicians who came together over the years to learn, perform, record and pass on my songs via the oral tradition, even when all I could do was to whistle the tunes.

(They probably don't need to be named, but among them are SFS Song Circle, Singing Alive, NW Folklife Festival, 50-strong international *Om Namah Shivaya* Chorus, SingPeace! Pilgrimage for Peace & Global Harmony, Dances of Universal Peace.)

1. Initiation

Coming of the Light

I am seated on the floor, across from a friend.
Her words float through my mind:
"Look for a place within,
entirely undisturbed by worldly care."

Such a place exists?

In what tiny recess of a body, which,
like so many piled-up mattresses,
bears the weight of the world?

Meanwhile, the mind casts its
ever-revolving beacon
on past, present and future,
reviewing a monumental list-
of-things-to-do
… and undo.

We sit for meditation,
the early morning rays of light
stream through lattice windowpanes.
Despair mounts on a wave of longing.

The voice of habit whispers:
'Don't let her see you cry.'
Eyes shut tightly
against a tidal wave of tears.
The body convulses and lets go.

C-R-A-C-K— a breaking sound in my chest.
Light blazes from the chasm of the heart.
Perfect peace replaces the desperate chaos—
the stormy seas of life, forever abated
in this dawn's pure light.

Moments later, climbing into my van,
I see the room in my mind's eye.
There, on a shelf in the corner
is a photo of her Guru,
her Baba.
I had not noticed him 'til now.
"Did you do that?"
I address him for the first time.
"Did you do that?"

My Initiation

"Om Namah Shivaya," we chant the mantra
in a darkened room.
I sit facing your photo.
"Help me, Baba!" I cry out silently to you.
I feel my body elongate —
at once ascending and slipping downward...
disappearing, or somehow vibrating
like a thousand-stringed instrument.
'This is going to be a good one,' I tell myself.

Now, in the place where I sit, the shape of a pewter pot,
its wide front opening reveals the same space within
and without.
An in-filling of divine elixir moves upward from toe to head.
I am suspended in an emulsion of love.
I am loved.

The mind spins in space somewhere to my left side:
"How could anyone do that? Where could they place their hands
to create such a sensation in my body?"
I tell myself: 'I'll never leave this spot!'
Yet, I open my eyes.
"I feel like I've just been made love to," I whisper wonderingly.

An air of intimate intoxication floods the room,
infecting my companions.
I go outside to join the others.
I cannot speak of what has taken place;
I know, somehow, it is sacred
and should not be tossed away on the wind.
Even so, I roll on the ground in pure ecstasy.

A cyclone has entered my spine.
The force of it has me lying on my back.
Only five of us attend this two-day workshop
at a small meditation center.
"How are you doing?" they ask.
"It's still going on!"
I am changed, and I know you have changed me.

For months, people bring me gifts, relics from Baba.
I look into the eyes of strangers and see only love.
Coming near to your photo,
I fall to the floor with intoxication,
and crawl out of bed at night to light a candle,
drowning again and again
in the ocean of your sweet nectar.

One Look

You recall the first time our eyes met?
You were entering the lobby from the elevator.
I held my daughter's hand
as we came down the stairs.
I whispered: "Baba."
You turned and held my gaze...

An eternity in an instant.

What did you do?
What did you see?

For me, "nothing" happened.
Yet, that first glance
remains seared in my memory
as the most impenetrable look
you ever gave me.

The Space Between

Baba,
I came to kneel near to you
in a quiet moment.

You kept your eyes on me,
while strains of an Indian raga
dissolved all limitations
of time and space.

As we met and merged
in the sound,
you gave an imperceptible nod,
and averted your gaze.

Making Way for the Lord

Making way for the Lord,
is the subject of this day,
my birthday.

Oh, God, refresh and gladden my spirit!
Let me purely receive your Infinite Bounty
on this day,
and all days, henceforth.
No hesitation.

Hold still, sister.
Absorb the divine presence,
feel the powerful, pulsing *shakti* within.
Feel the heat of God's love in your heart.

Who is it,
if it is not you,
Pushkara?

At some point—
and why not now?
I have to get it,
that God has visited
the profound gift of his loving light,
His own life,
upon me.

God's Bounty
is my inheritance.
And my guru
has awakened me to it.

Curious God

Curious God!
You've made Your way
into all of my affairs.

Like an unwelcome guest,
You've burst in on me,
even while I am still asleep,
or napping.

Is there no "right-to-privacy," here?
I run to hide.
You follow,
and get there first.

Do You have eyes in the back of Your head?
How else would You know
my every thought
and motion?

Peering into closets,
You hold up bits of dirty laundry—
little lies, evasive deceptions, nervous habits—
strewn there.
"See?"

I'm embarrassed,
but not yet ready
to concede the point.
I wonder,
"Why can't You mind Your own business?"

Then, at the crack of dawn,
for a brief, lucid moment,
I drop the pretense.

The eye that sees
is the "I"
that is
Me.

Curious God!

His Song

It seems a new identity
is standing by, awaiting me.

I feel its nearness deep inside.
In times of calm, it does confide.

Awareness of its purity,
an all-in-one,"
no "you," nor "me."

Being-ness, replete yet simple,
God, at home, in my heart's temple.

Strumming, now, He holds the lute,
absorbed in sound, bliss absolute.

And in His rapture
where am "I?"

His song of Love,
His breath...
a sigh.

2. Sadhana, the Path

Find Out about the Voice

"Find out about the voice," my guru said.
"Somebody must know something.
And when you do, let me know,
because we can all learn."

Disbelieving, I'd seen many who knew nothing.
But this was my guru's command,
setting me on a course.
The voice would heal.

"Totally," the astrologer said,
"but in relation to letting the Lord do the healing.
As you align yourself with God's will,
and commit yourself to the work you are meant to do,
the voice will work perfectly."

"It's not the voice, it's the heart," the psychic healer said,
"Open your heart. Become your heart."

"I can't find it," I said.
Below a wound in the earth is a swirling dark pool
in this space of the heart.

"Dive for it," the inner voice said.
"Raise it, slowly, with utmost care and patience.
One cannot love without a heart."

Gentle lotus, floating upward to the light.
"I can't breathe," I said. "There's a rock in my chest."

"How can you get love from a rock?"
the inner voice said.

"You can see the rays of the Self
through a broken heart," my guru once said.

Lord, break open my heart?

Sword of Longing

Must I always live with this sword in my chest?
Even to want to know God,
to face Him alone,
without seeking others' support,
the heart must be freed of such pain.
Lord, why do You
continue to punish me?

I cannot chant my guru's name aloud,
nor do I remember it but seldom.
Yet, to catch even a glimpse of her form,
to hear a fragment of another's
tale of yearning,
this voice chokes back
a certain cry of anguish.
Hot tears swell and splash over my cheeks,
and that sword renews its initial wound—
from within.
This is my daily experience.

My guru's voice is my life's breath;
she is my dear one.
Her eyes beam rays of sunlight.
Her smile is love's beckoning.
This much I know of her.
But that part of her,
that is within me
cannot be recovered.

Rather, it is a breath that won't breathe,
a cry that won't sound,
a love that longs for itself,
that has made me its companion.

Lord, where is your mercy?
The skin is beginning to wrinkle
and slide from my face.
The back is paining.
The gait is less spry.
Time grows short.

Do I need any other qualification,
than this infernal longing
to know God as my own Self?

Simultaneity

Baba, I didn't want to walk the dog.
          Baba, you are the silence.

It was raining last night.
I wanted to argue about the dog.

          The ever-present support,
          the living grace,
          the core, of my existence.

There was no give, no surrender,
here in my heart.

          You love me, because you can't help it.
          and I can't stop loving you.

In the morning, I dusted off my altar.
and I sit here beside it,
weeping...
out of love
for you.

          This fact, alone
          is the cause
          of our union,
          and the source
          of my salvation.

The fist releases,
turning to open
like a flower
in sunlight.

Tug of War

Tug-of-war?
Wrenching conflict,
bewildering indecision.

Where did I lose my soul?
Tucked into a bunting—
sh-h-h-h-h-h...
My mind is sleeping.

Schizoid scare,
life-fire revered,
snuffed in fragile grains.
Sifted fragments,
cooled.

Solid, salad, sullen, saline, silly, sally, souly,
pider, powder, budder, bade her, sadder,
manner, ermine, never, erstwhile, legend,
generous, nerve gas, assassin, sandwich, anathema.

Anesthesia.

Requiem for a Fighter

My insides feel like jelly.
I'm scared silly.
This year's astrological menu?
"Crucifixion of the ego-centered existence."
Fried chicken.

I mean, have I ever really let go?
Taken the leap?
It's been more like slow death,
like skin ripped from bone,
peeled back, layer by layer.
What is that aphorism? That "suture?"
"The pain that is yet to come
can and should be…"
Enjoyed, is it?

So, I'll tell you how I do it.
I'll tell you exactly how I do it.
Listen, I pick a fight with God!
It's like this:
God lays it out like it is, see.
And I come back with:
"No, no, I've got a better idea."

Yeah, I learned that from my mother.
She had a chip on her shoulder—
about God, I mean.
I didn't like her way, either,
so, I had to fight with her, too.
But I learned a few tricks from her, you know.

Fighting is a way of life
for a basically conflictual nature.
It's a way of feeling alive
while remaining dead...
to the Truth.
Yeah.
I got that from my mother.

A lot of my battles have been waged
during *Shri Guru Gita.*
You might not think of a chant as a battleground,
but if you're gonna keep a war on with God,
it's the best.
You can feel like a real hero—
wounded in battle—the purple heart.

First, there's the body.
Sitting in a steady posture for one and a half hours
in the early hours of the morning!
At that hour, the body isn't even awake,
to say nothing of limber!
So, that kept us busy for a few years.

Then, we learned nodding out.
Oh, the bliss of drifting
into a drowsy samadhi.
Then, God whispered,
"You need to do something more."

I admit, I got curious.
I took the bait.
I was gonna learn *Shri Guru Gita*,
word for word,
down to writing the Sanskrit
in Devanagari script.
To keep myself awake, I'd start off with verse 5,
and translate every fifth verse.

The guru had been away from the ashram in India for a month.
She was gonna be away another five weeks.
I was congratulating myself
for finding something just for me—
private, you know—
and she walks in the gate that very day!

Verse 5: "The guru is indeed *Brahman*."
As we gather around her in the courtyard,
every word, every glance,
even the slightest flick of a finger,
sets the universe in motion.
It was her idea all along, her *prasad*.

Well, to tell the truth,
I didn't get it right off.
It took her turning up somewhere during my day,
everyday,
to bring back the day's verse,
and show its exact meaning for me.

What was it? Verse 35?
"You are my father, my mother, my brother, my God…"
That was the day I was sweeping
the second floor corridor of the dorm.
"I really need a mother," I'm telling myself.
"But I already have a mother.
She did the best she could,
was dedicated to her job.
It's just that she couldn't take me
farther than she herself had gone."

"What would it be like
to have a divine Mother?" I wonder.
By morning *darshan* time,
I'm really curious.
She—you know who I mean—
is sitting in the courtyard.
I go up in the line thinking,
"I don't know, I don't know."

So, I bow and look up
to see her reaching over to her side table.
There's a tiny crystal bud vase
that tilts to one side like a cornucopia
with two tiny feet for balance.
As I rise up, she begins to caress
the rose it holds.
Such perfect care.

I go back to my seat, close my eyes, and *bam!*
There's that bud vase—
a vision taking up my whole chest.
"Is it a lotus, is it a lotus?"
My name means "lotus," see.

Anyway, the verse comes to me,
"You are my father…"
I get that father and mother are the creator,
the brother, the sustainer,
and God, the unifier,
and dissolver of the universe.

Now, my inner voice declares:
"I want to walk with my brother."
It's her, see.
A moment's hesitation.
Then, I walk out into the courtyard
and wait for the guru.
Twenty more people show up out of the blue
to take her *darshan.*

Meanwhile, I'm standing like a dummy
out in the middle of nowhere,
while the guard directs traffic around me.
All I know is that I need to trust that inner voice,
to take a dare.

She walks down the steps,
slips her shoes on,
and walks over to me.
I fall in with her, and we begin
to walk toward her door.

Suddenly, she throws her arm across my chest.
Addressing someone nearby in Hindi,
she points overhead.
As she speaks, her three fingers—middle man, ring and pinkie—
come to rest on my upper arm,
where she pushes gently,
opening out my heart.

Next, she takes a step or two
to the tree well,
where a red and white striped amaryllis
stands in full bloom.
She places the same three fingers
against one of its petals.
With her index finger,
she strokes the long yellow stamen.
I get it.

As she enters her door,
two girls are talking excitedly,
"Did you see the way she stroked the flower?"
I mean, everyday was like that!
Exquisite.

Well, she got me awake.
Then, it was the mind's turn.
I mean, we don't know war
'til we take on the mind, right?
"You should!"
"I can't."
"You will."
"Why me?"
"You're a jerk, a dummy, no good."
"No, no, don't say that!"
"You can't do anything right!"
"Poor me."
I'd rather be sleeping.
(Sing to the tune: "On Top of Old Smokey.")

I tried getting sick.
If you can't get out of bed
to make it to the war zone,
who's gonna fault you for that?
I took a little vacation.
"I just need a rest.
The change'll do me some good."

Cheap tricks, all of 'em, I admit.
I was trying to outsmart God.
"What is this pain in my chest?"

The moment of Truth,
the golden opportunity,
came in the fall:
I got the message:
It's almost 1990.
Resolve to show up, sit up straight,
and stay awake.
Keep your eyes focused on the text,
and your ears tuned to the chant.

How she got me praying
for that one-pointed focus,
I'll never know.
Musta had my guard down, hunh?
Or maybe I lost interest in the stakes.
The argument seems so petty, right?

Anyway, along about *Diwali*, the Indian New Year,
—what is that, November?—
I got desperate, losing my grip.
If there was a rock in the road,
I'd stub my toe on it—
not once, not twice,
but every time I went that way.
Even if I planned to go another way,
I'd find myself
stumbling over the same rock,
making the same fool mistake over and over.

It's like there was this weakness in me,
wanting to make a fool out of me,
wanting to turn me into a loser.

I heard it, maybe for the first time:
"Think on me alone."
"Think only of the guru."
It's there in *Shri Guru Gita*
seems like a hundred times.
This was not some high-flown esoteric maneuver.
I plain ran out of ideas.
It was survival, really.
I'm like a dead soldier, rising up
and walking off the battlefield.

At *Diwali,*
that's when I made my new year's resolution—
to think only of the guru.
Maybe it was a prayer,
maybe a promise,
maybe both.

Let me tell you something.
I don't feel
like a human punching-bag anymore.
There's a rock-solid,
steady pillar of strength
that holds me from inside.
Sometimes it seems like the Washington Monument,
a *Shiva lingam,* a safe harbor.

It supports a tender, blossoming devotion:
the willingness
to walk her sword's edge
to nowhere that I know.
A true warrior needs to know
where and when and how to wage war.

Listen to this:
the guru works her will,
not by waging war with what is,
but through absolute surrender to it.

Pig

Closed my eyes for a split second
during *Shri Guru Gita*.
Saw a squealing pig in a pen,
darting this way and that,
trying frantically to get out.

I recognized that pig.

Me,
trying to get some words out onto this page.

And I laughed at myself—
for the first time in twenty-four hours.

Ants

There's an ant walking upside down
on this glass tabletop.

At this morning's *Guru Gita*,
I looked down at the marble floor.
An ant was making its own way to somewhere.
I have never before
felt reverence for an ant.

I have a new *seva*—
supervising spices for the kitchen.
We're located under the trees—
like the ants.

After my first day, yesterday,
I heard my inner voice.
It said: "The karma of the voice may be finished."
I felt like a kid
who couldn't wait to open her presents—
and peeked.

I have so much to say.
It's all crowding up around my throat,
like sunlight dancing on the crest of a wave.
It can't all come out at once.

Or can it?

Only when the words that keep my story alive
dissolve in the sea of pure awareness
is there the faintest possibility
of freeing my heart from my throat.

Careful.
This is where the attention gets caught
in the nets of delusion.
Sure. The mind moves,
like water in a bathtub—
rippling one direction 'til it hits the side,
then, going off in another direction.

The walls are there.
The flow appears to be blocked.
Only now, nothing can stop this flooding.
The tide that went out
a long time ago,
is rolling in—
wave after wave—
upon the shores
of my awakening consciousness.

Don't look now.
It's rolling over you.
You who?
Yoo hoo! ♫
I hear an echo.

We're all riding the same wave
in a glass-bottomed boat.
Ants.

Nobody's Home
(Song)

Refrain:
It's nobody's home where the floor's never clean,
where dust lies thick on shelves, fans and screen.
This is a place where everyone's said:
"I do my part; I sweep under my bed!"

But how did you get from your bed to the door?
Did you notice the tracks
that you've left there before?
Instead of "I can,"
the mantra, "I can't"
casts shadows of gloom.
It's a heart-sickened chant.

And sick you've become, and sick you will stay,
lying around on your sick bed all day,
until you can see that the bed you are on
rests on the floor in the house
of the great holy one.

(Refrain)

From bed to door, and wall to wall,
this floor reaches bath and terrace and hall,
and free box and stairs and courtyard and walk.
This floor sees no boundaries;
the floor knows no block.

From this point of view,
it is our support.
Its generosity never falls short.
It gives and it gives of itself without end,
never asking for much,
like the love of a friend.

So, pick up a broom, a dust cloth, a mop;
make this house a home,
scrubbed from bottom to top.
Love comes full circle and makes room for more,
where each lends a hand
in keeping the floor.

(Refrain)

All in a Day's Sadhana

Stepping into the shower:
"*Shri Guru Gita* is not only the body of the guru.
It is the guru-disciple relationship."

All these years not noticing:
one-and-a-half hours
private *darshan* each day:
dialogue, inner revelation,
moments of perfect repose,
challenges to action,
ecstasy.
It's been the lens through which I've come to see,
and to understand my Self.

Now, silently following the text:
"Please, my guru, illumine *Shri Guru Gita*
as the guru-disciple relationship."

Loneliness is burning a hole in my chest.
I've reached the limits of my ability,
and interest
in going on alone.
I need people.

Let me understand the principle of "relatedness."
There's no difference
between the guru-disciple relationship
and "the world"— people.
As there, so here — the same blocks appear.
The dam of emotional denial bursts
in floods of hot tears
that carry memories,
even from infancy.

A light breakfast:
"My guru, I don't exist here in this ashram.
Only that which is illumined by your love
exists, is seen, valued, and loved by others.
Shine your ever-lovin' light on me."

The head wants to duck;
the eyes cast downward.
"No! Stop! This is not my light
that shines through my eyes.
It is my guru's light.
Let them see it."

The same love within me
exists within you.
I promise not to hide my pure love from other people.
I lift my head.

I walk on the circular cinder path,
a knot of pain in my heart.
I can't breathe.
It's the way I stopped the hurt.
It eventually stopped the voice.
"I did this to myself!"
That was then; this is now.
The karma of the voice will end.

Meditating silently
before the altar of my grandfather guru,
I follow an impulse to go to a class instead.
If the world is love; let me love the world.
"I need other people!" I tell myself.
As a group, we dive deep together.

Now, I sit in the sun on a quiet perch,
overlooking a stretch of lawn.
I struggle to write lines
to make myself understood.
I feel blocked.
Reflecting "Journaling is so easy
when I write solely for my guru."

I stand, to leave my perch,
and see my guru walking toward me
flanked by teens and assorted others.
I find a spot and await her there,
praying to be open,
to let down my barriers to the guru-disciple relationship.
A wall of love moves through me.

Following the evening chant,
my heart feels bereft,
crying out for what it already has.
Even while living in love,
practicing the art of true love in the world,
the mind does not recognize it.
In relatedness, there is no "relationship."

Another of the mind's paper tigers
brought to its knees.
It's all in a day's *sadhana*.

Life after Death?

Loneliness is a hot spear.
It burns through to the heart
where muffled cries are sounding.

Wave upon wave
of tortured longing
rolls through the body.
Memory flashes,
fueling flames of feeling.
Aching tears splash
from eyes shut against others' detection.

This is not the first time.
It's another ego death.
This death has hovered, now,
for twenty years or so,
rising and falling in intensity.

Is there life after death?

Birth-Day

In the life of the mind,
there are many births, many deaths,
while the soul has no beginning, no end.
It is eternal, unchanging.
Spiritual initiation is the birth of life
outside the mind;
it is the gift of eternal life.

It is said, initiation takes place only once in a lifetime.
Yet, Self-recognition may come
like a slowly breaking dawn,
as imperceptible shifts of light, color, and form,
arranged on an invisible screen.

Initiation is the gift of the gracious,
"un-understood Mother."
Sadhana is the nurture of her offspring
from infancy until, as a mature mind,
one assumes a steady posture
in the Self.

Like a toddler reaching for a doorknob
just outside its grasp,
I am stretching to open the door
of a closed mind.
I feel a birth taking place within me,
a birth into the spiritual life.

The inner voice informs:
"It's mine now," as I approach the guru's chair.
A simultaneous inner movement
grounds, de-mystifies, and empowers.
As if standing on my own two spiritual legs
for the first time,
I know that liberation
and the means to it,
are now mine.

Is this the dawn of Self-recognition?
Is this the first acknowledgment of the inner guru?
My own Self?
No longer sentenced to the confines of my mind,
I am free to practice
purno a'ham vimarsha,
the perfect "I" awareness.

The shapes and forms
of old habits and past karmas
remain as shadowy impressions
in a small corner
of the screen of available consciousness.
No more assuming center stage and top billing,
all things come to one
who merely resolves
to "think on the guru alone,"
and sometimes remembers.

Gifts of Sadhana

I wear the gifts of *sadhana*
in a garland about my shoulders.
Lord, which of these rare blooms
shall I offer at Your feet?

3. In Search of a Voice

Breathing Life into Death

What can anyone say
when we are all
holding our breath,
this way?

Is it grief,
or holding on to it,
that squeezes the heart so?

If our only hope of relief
is in letting go,
and that doesn't work,
all is lost.
Isn't it?

There's no help
in this infernal waiting...
not knowing, not daring
to give voice
to what is.

But remember?

Before this time,
we knew—
and understood—
the great secret:

That life
is a gift.

And breathing,
in time…
together…
is our good fortune.
Though we never knew
before we came
that we would receive
so much.

Breathe, breathe.
Breathe life into death,
for in this exchange—
one life's breath for another—
grief gives way…
to gratitude.

Transition—1968

Woman-child, who are you?

I am.
I am child.
I am becoming woman.

Frightened,
I seek the image
of gentle strength,
of protective warmth,
from shattering defeat,
and overwhelming challenge.

Child am I,
who contracts inward and down,
in the put-down, grown-up world
of infinite hurt.
Whining, hiding, seething behind
walls of sleep, laughter and docility.

But woman I am and am becoming.
Up and through and outward,
a reaching into life,
a reaching-out for love, trust.

Flushed and awakened,
I seek the reality of sensual communion,
of exploding consciousness.
Conceived and nurtured within me,
a new being stirs and breathes.

Transition—1973

"I hear you're a woman now. How is it?"

"Well, I'm not sure.
I'm working at it only part-time."

"I guess it takes some getting used to."

"Yeah, at times I wonder how I ever got myself into this."

"You must have wanted the job, though."

"That's true. I'm always biting off more than I can chew."

"You think you'll take the job next year?"

"Oh, I feel like I've started something I want to finish."

"Don't overdo it, dear; take it easy on yourself."

"I have to keep reminding myself of that.
It's getting easier, though.
I think the first year's the hardest.
Don't you?"

It Takes So Long

It takes so long
to even want to become one's own person—
to feel complete within oneself.
So many years have passed
in handing the old umbilical to this or that one:
"Here, would you hold this for me?"

So many moments have been lost in feeling,
"I must have left something behind."
Or in looking "over there"
for that which can be known only
when all of the strands of one's awareness
come to rest within one's own being,
within the Self.

In wanting to know that wholeness,
one gives up all ideas,
even the impulse to nurture ideas.
For, from ideas—desires—
spring activity.
And from activity, unrest.
And from unrest,
blindness to the Truth.

Pull Taffy

I wanna say what's in my soul,
bring together those strewn-around bits
of imperfection, non-permission, and suffering.
Make a pull-taffy out of 'em,
make 'em sing,
change their shapes,
make 'em sweet,
like something
anybody'd like to taste—like CANDY!

So, I can eat 'em
and push 'em out the other end.
Same brown-golden color,
but not sticking to my hands.

Then we can get on with the show.

Out of Time

They say: "Time waits for no man,"
and death awaits us all.
I died to the world again today,
and mourned my own passing—
though, at the time,
I didn't know what I was crying about.

So, I ask you,
"How, then, does a dead man live?"
I can tell you how he should not—
not, that is, if he seeks eternal life, true repose.
He does not indulge in sense pleasures
nor court the six enemies
nor chase desires...
He doesn't start anything he can't finish.

But, if this is so—
and I believe it to be—
what does he do with all the time he has on his hands?
What does he think, if he's not making plans?
Where does he go? What does he say?
What is his state? How does he play?

And how does he hold steady
in the truth,
that what is the "stuff of life" for some
is "dead meat" to the noble ones?

I've died before to desire,
but the long fingers of attachment
wrapped themselves even more tightly
around their objects,
clouding the hope
that it's over.
Finished.

The mind is not totally convinced.
It argues with itself.
Now, the feelings charge onto the scene
and the raging fires of existence
blaze once again.

My Lord says what's right here in front of me
is not Real
and that something I cannot see or comprehend
has built this fire.
Through worship of the Lord alone,
it will be quenched.

To be continued… I am out of time.

What Does the Madness Want?
(Song, adapted from the work of John Gorka)

[Snap fingers]

Refrain:
B. B. King was wrong:
the thrill, it isn't gone.
The thrill, it is here; it is now; it is strong.
The thrill, it isn't gone; the thrill, it isn't gone.
The thrill, it is here; it is now; it is strong.
The thrill, it isn't gone.
That means B. B. King was wrong.
Whoa, whoa.

[Syncopate with lines of song]

The madness wants to dance.
The madness wants to play.
It makes its own music,
lives inside each day.

(*Refrain*)

Sat-chid-ananda,
being, conscious and bliss;
Self-contained and Self-completing,
life seals its kiss.

(*Refrain*)

[Instrumental break]

The madness wants a partner.
"Going to the dance?"
The one is two;
two will be one.
No one escapes love's glance.

Coming alive above the waist,
above the forehead's eye,
revealing, "the Madness" laughing there,
into his arms I fly.
That means...

(*Refrain*)

Smiles

A short sound escapes my lips as,
alight in the early morning sun,
a hummingbird comes to dance.
It whirrs into sight,
swings to and fro, suspended at *Nataraj's* elbow,
flits across his chest, and flings itself into thin air.
I turn to meet the mirror
of my open-mouthed delight—
the eyes of another witness to this blessing,
smiling into mine.

I circumambulate Lord *Ganesha,*
the remover of obstacles,
arranged on the ground in colored sand.
Turning to gaze down at his image,
I watch two tiny chipmunks
dash from nearby underbrush to take his *darshan,*
scampering away in opposite directions.
I look up,
into the amused face across the *rangoli,*
exchanging a smile.

This day began with a smile!
Chanting before dawn,
my mind moves from mental worship,
just a fraction of an inch—from seeing to being—
to merge in the infinite.
I am inside, where Lord *Shiva*
is all smiles!

A warm current of love
draws me toward an old friend.
We stand side by side,
to perform *arati* for the true guru,
for the beloved best of gurus.
The light of her glory
beams from our hearts through our smiles.

The sign reads:
"Please help yourself to a rose."
Smiling down at the woman behind the desk,
I lift an old-fashioned pink rose
from its nest in the little basket.
"You can have more," she tells me.
I spot a friend and take another to offer her.
Our sharing reflects the richness,
the inner smile.

A sweet smile plays all day
across the petals of my heart.
I move toward the temple, now,
to chant the evening *arati*.
A friend—in silence—sits quietly, reading.
I whistle a greeting.
He looks up.
We wave smiling "hello" in each other's direction.

Walking out toward the lake,
I catch a glimpse of a bunny and a chipmunk,
hopping to the same tune
underneath low branches.
I feel the same softness in the smile
of another passerby.

Those in white at a week-long course
chant at sunset above the lake.
Rounding the lake with a friend,
I point silently overhead
at broad, fanning rays of white and dark light,
shooting upward from clouds
outlined in brilliant gold.
It takes our breath away.
We grin together at our good fortune.

It's that subtle surrender,
from standing on the outside
to being in it,
that brings a smile to the heart,
expanding to show itself
in playful,
everyday and breathtaking ways.
This smile *is* our destiny—
and it's for keeps!

4. Awakening to Love

No "Other"

Don't you recognize me?
Many lives and many coverings
have made us forget
our promise to each other.
We do not know one another
by the faces we wear.
Pray for the eyes of the heart
to be opened.

Do you think,
just because our eyes do not meet,
our bodies do not touch,
that you can escape my ministrations
of love?
What is given of God
is received of God.

God, help me.
This one who was given in love
has forgotten himself.
Only in the dark
can a true husband
pass by his own wife
awaiting him
by the door.

Love's desire leads me near to you
and holds me stupefied
in its intoxicating liqueur.
"Are you all right?" you whisper.
"I don't know."
I'm doing my "homework."
We both dissolve.

For that brief moment,
love is all that exists.

An Offering

Om Guru.

Love brews and foams in my heart.
Is it an abscess,
or is it cosmic effervescence?
I can scarcely tell the difference.

I know this:
that I do it to myself.
From the Self,
for the Self.

I seek consummation:
flesh against flesh,
mind within mind,
oblivion in soul union.

With *him*, Lord?
Can we simply storm the gates,
give love, passion, and joy,
full rein—
no rules,
utter abandonment?

Keshav, darling, no!
Don't throw up the road blocks to Love.
You cite rules, stand back and
recite the scriptural injunctions:
avoid desire, passion, sex, lust...

Jump headlong into it,
and you will leave all the six enemies
and their kin in the dust.
Parade around the edges,
patrol the gates,
and surely,
you succeed only
in perpetuating the argument.

Come! Fly to me.
Yield.
Surrender.
My arms,
my soul,
open to receive you.

For Keshav

Love's relics,
close, upon my altar,
in a red, China-silk box—
long since grief had come and gone.

Wedding band,
silver anniversary phoenix rising—
earrings, necklace, the strand of carved silver beads,
tossed out to sea.

Why? Only today,
casting from the end of the fishing pier,
and watching them sink
beneath the sunlit waves...

Why? Did I not see,
except in this farewell,
through tender tears,
the obstacles in their worship?

I release them, now.
May all God's blessings be yours.
May all God's blessings be mine.
Our karma is cleared and balanced.

Twelve years on the shelf.
Love's promise opens wide this box.
I have slipped aside
the bone ivory clasp.
Within, it's you, O Love,
I wish to honor, now,
with green stones of healing—
mala, ring.

And tiny sapphires—
your starlit eyes in miniature.
Look, Love, temple water,
yajna ash, *samadhi* soil.

Come now, Love,
accept this heart-shaped brooch.
It holds our guru's sacred song,
and the petal from a rose placed on her head.

In this, true love's dawning,
I prepare these gifts,
and my heart,
to receive you, here.

In my guru's love, I am your own.

Discarded

Moon snail shells
lie humped along the surface
of sand at low tide.

He picks his way among them,
lifting, turning each to admire
its unique form and coloration.
He gathers many in a bag
to carry from the shore.

Laying them out on the deck,
again, he admires each shell.
Selecting a few,
he carefully places them in a shoe box
to take home with him.
The rest, like me, he leaves behind.

Discarded?
Or put aside for some future use?

In Your Presence

My approach to you, bolder in some ways
than I had ever allowed myself to be,
was a step in my own birthing process.
And loving, learning more about loving—
openly, deeply, generously...selfishly,
immersing myself in my own experience:
I am pain, I am longing, I am fear.

I am.

Deepening and expanding my being
in your presence.
Now, ending.

Gifts of your presence,
of staying, coming back to, working through—
yielding our Self, one to the other.
No more.

Dying a little—
holes in my heart and belly.
Having nothing left to lose,
I give in to feelings overflowing,
and to the promise of renewal.

For the price of holding back,
of softening my commitment
to myself and to our friendship
is too great to pay.
I would rather die
to be reborn
than not to have lived at all.

This is my cry of mourning,
my song of friendship
in your presence.

Knowing that endings are different each time,
not knowing what this ending will be;
feeling only the holes in my being
that were once filled
by knowing you were there.

Holding on, now letting go—
I have nothing to say.
What is you that is inside of me,
remains and sustains that which is given
in your presence.

Our All-Over Love

Drifting seas of sleep and waking,
my eyes light upon your cheek.
I feel its subtle warmth so near to mine.
Your knowing eyes in sidewise glance
tease love's urges
out of their hiding places.

I wonder, "Do you know?"
Are you really with me
in this phantom meeting?
Or is this one more autistic tragedy
cast ashore life's Isolation Isle?

The answer comes in tender waves—
ebbing, flowing, rolling motions,
perfectly timed, exquisitely placed.
I open wide my boat,
wider still,
willing this super-sensuous tide.

You have a way of entering.
Our all-over love infills me with ecstasy.
As long as your presence lingers,
I won't move far from these sacred sands.
Don't be surprised to find me combing this beach
for any sign of you.

5. Family

Daddy
(Song)

Daddy sat me on his knee,
eyes were bugged, all watery;
nearly suffocated by his breath
so strong with booze.
"Ever see a thousand-dollar bill?"
he boasted, I remember still,
though the roll he flashed
was one week's wages of his crew.

Refrain:

Oh, Daddy, where were you
when I was growing old and only ten years old,
holding hurt inside me with no place else to go?
Like you, I learned the lethal art
of hiding pain inside my heart,
and caged the song bird there so long ago.

One night he heard us giggling,
broke into the room and left a sting,
and by my heels he hung me upside down
in helpless shame.
He beat me there until I cried:
"No, Daddy, no! I'll be good next time."
What child's crime committed there,
equals the punishment that came?

By then, my sister, Marj, and I
sent signals back and forth as spies,
whenever one of us saw Daddy coming.
If he was drunk, we'd imitate:
bug out our eyes, match his gait.
It was a joke between us
that also served as warning.

(Refrain)

Dad's kid sis was my heroine,
until the day, while drunk on gin,
she pulled me close to whisper venom in my ear.
Breath rank, speech slurred,
to me she purred:
"Men will always want you, dear."
Stamped "marked woman" on me then and there.

Indeed, they touched me here and there,
in the halls, on the stairs:
blocked my path, cornered me,
played with me upon their knee.
Once, while talking on the phone,
Uncle Herb, all hot and stoned,
lunged toward the bed
and made a dive right for me.

Why is this game played silently?
I kicked to ward him off, you see,
but held "our secret" without ever telling.
And in my heart concealed the mark:
the truth that I was dark,
was bad, because another tried to hurt me.

(Refrain)

That year, the Rosenbergs were dead,
and the Party lived in dread.
My father's drinking led to our expulsion.
Once more sworn to secrecy,
the stakes were high: life and death, you see.
Now the walls began to close in all around me.

They took away my best friend.
I could no longer see nor send
a message to her,
not one word of farewell.
With lips sealed against the pain,
wounds to the heart, again, again.
In exile, I grew old and died while living.

(Refrain)

These untold stories of the self,
lay thirty years upon the shelf,
until I saw my life
come crashing down around my ears.

"God, help me," I cried inwardly.
How could I guess it'd set him free?
From that day, he never took another drink.
Been sober all these years.

Now, Daddy's only ten years-old.
He lost the rest to alcohol,
but I can see that, in his way,
he's doing fine.

This song is not for him, you see.
I'm searching for the Truth in me,
a way to let the feelings be that I had left behind.

With no one there to comfort me,
I blamed myself, and could not feel
the feelings that my words are now expressing.
A child's song to God, never sung:
I'll sing it 'til the hurt is gone,
so I can let the past go with my blessing.

Oh, Daddy, where were you
when I was growing old and all alone,
holding hurt inside me
with no place else to go?
Like you, I learned the lethal art
of hiding pain inside my heart,
and caged the song bird there so long ago.

Ironic Tonic
(Song)

Refrain:
I'm graduated, emancipated,
I'm an educated fool,
'cause tomorrow I get out and pound the streets,
join the rat race and the car pool.

Well, they say that bein' a mother
is the fulfillment of womanhood,
but in talkin' around, there're some hitches I've found
that no other than a mother understood.

(Refrain)

Ten years of teachin' twenty,
as if three wasn't enough
to drive me to drink; couldn't hear myself think,
singin' "Diamonds in the Rough."

(Refrain)

On the last leg of my journey,
wanting something more from this life,
went to the ivory tower for ego, money, and power,
a liberated teacher, mother, and wife.
And now...

(Refrain)

Child of Body; Child, My Soul

Child of body and child of mind,
I cut the cord of ties that bind.

When did I ever just let you be?
Have you known yourself apart from me?

Why did I ask so much from you
and give so little of the love that's true?

What greed have I that I want more
and would bar your passage to that other shore?

A silent voice, a bitter rage, in cold-blood ink,
upon the page.

I dig a hole and light the flame,
burn words of grief and call your name.

I release you, now; I set you free—
to live as you, and not for me.

And to my Self return a power,
so lightly given at your birth hour.

With my hand, I make a sword
and sever there the unseen cord.

Through the lens of my mind's eye,
I hold your form up to the sky.
In swaddling light, this child, now grown,
as infant comes, returning home.

Child of body; child, my soul.

Sunburst

O sunburst!
Darling daughter
cast your glow
upon the water.

Rippling rays
at daybreak gleaming,
over waves,
love's light sent streaming.

Unbounded joy
inside your laughter
echoes forth
and ever after.

Precious life
Behold your glory,
Sing your song!
Yes, tell your story.

Gift of God,
O jewel, my pleasure,
will you know,
and share…
your treasure?

6. Community, Friendship & Gratitude

Meeting

We meet on this serpent path,
you and I,
to stroll side by side —
your arm encircling my waist.

Assuming myriad guises, numberless forms,
we must have enacted untold dramas,
fought many battles,
seeded and birthed countless children—
of both body and mind.

Look!
From our present vantage point,
the spiraling course
embraces all that we are,
all that we have ever been.

I'm happy to be here with you.
So familiar you seem:
your gentle touch, the sound of your voice.
I see my Self in the transparency
of your face and smiling eyes.

Alone, we have taken many steps
to arrive here together.
Again.

We pause to catch our breath,
and warm ourselves in the sun.
Then, smiling, we move higher,
to follow the circling way, less known.

Aren't You Glad!

(Song for Mother & Father Divine,
Peace Mission Movement)

Praise be His name!

Aren't you glad!

In form He came,

Aren't you glad!

and married there,

Aren't you glad!

a bride so fair.

Aren't you glad!

Refrain:
Sing,
Aren't you glad!
Aren't you glad!
Aren't you glad! (Repeat)

Heaven on earth,
Aren't you glad!
Christ to His church,
Aren't you glad!
with humankind,
Aren't you glad!
union divine,
Aren't you glad!

(Refrain)

Life in the Lord,
Aren't you glad!
I am made whole.
Aren't you glad!
Becoming one,
Aren't you glad!
lead me home,
Aren't you glad!

(Refrain)

82

In Unseen Ways

*For Multifaith AIDS Project residents,
staff & volunteers*

In unseen ways, I am your sister.
In my dream,
my friend drives a VW bug.
I sit in the passenger seat beside him.
We turn onto a busy campus street,
people crisscrossing in every direction.

A young couple passes by,
arms wrapped around the other's waist,
talking excitedly to each other.
Oblivious to everything and everyone around them,
they ride side by side in battery-powered wheelchairs.

I recognize them.
We wave and call back and forth,
shouting over the heads of the people passing by,
subjects most folks keep private.
What does it matter?
People may hear the words, but they don't understand.

In unseen ways, I am your sister.
For sixteen years, I could not speak.
Wrapped in a cocoon of isolation,
a life worth little to me.
With each fresh loss, I died some more:
voice, marriage, home, family, job, money…
Few know death as a condition of life.
I died many times over and lived on.

I cried out: "God help me!"
A spark of life ignited.
I watched it grow.
It burned away self-hate and fearful doubt.
It spoke: "I am Love," it said.

In unseen ways, I am your sister.
This light brought me to you.
For you, too, are that love,
nothing but love.

Nine months have passed since we first met,
a challenging, pregnant time for all.
Births and deaths intertwined.
Releasing the old, embracing the new,
we will go on.

We Can All Be Better

(Song sent to President Bill Clinton, 1996)

Refrain:
We can all be better,
move it on up to the light.
And there is enough love
in one human heart to make it right.

What did our forefathers say,
on that Declaration Day?
"These truths we hold to be self-evident:
all men are equal under God,"
And they signed it into law.
They got the democratic process underway.

Refrain:
And we can make it better,
move it on up to the light.
And there is enough love
in one human heart to make it right.

Four score and seven years, hence, he stood,
where brothers fought and died at Gettysburg,
Abe said, "This nation, under God,
shall take new birth."
"A land conceived in liberty,
all men being equal, should be free.
A government of the people,
by the people, for the people
shall not perish from this earth."

Refrain:
We knew we had to make it better,
move it on up to the light.
And there is enough love
in one human heart to make it right.

Now, for two hundred years and more,
our work and watchword, as before:
"*E pluribus unum*—out of many we are one."
With President Bill and Hillary,
torchbearers for democracy,
in the pre-dawn of the new millennium.

Refrain:
We can make it better,
move it on up to the light.
And there is enough love
in one human heart to make it right.

Political opponents are astounded,
and the analysts, confounded,
at Bill's resilience to bounce back time and again.
He started out a politician,
but the office holds a mission,
to lead this country and the world
where none have been.

Refrain:
If we all pull together,
move it on up to the light.
And there is enough love
in one human heart to make it right.

Bill said: "And by a faith we all are bound,
the relentless search for common ground,
to those who seek to bridge their own divides,
we hear the call."

"We pledge allegiance to this land;
to the principles on which it stands.
One world, under God, indivisible,
with liberty and justice for all."

Refrain:
We have come so far together,
move it on up to the light.
And there is enough love
in one human heart to make it right.

Community of Great Souls
(For Dr. Wayne Larrabee, plastic surgeon & poet)

Laugh with me,
but do not disparage
my speech of thanks and praise.
Supinely delivered from behind a mask—
—I admit, a smidge inebriated—
I look up at you and the others
there, in the surgical operating theater.

Anesthesia, we know, dulls feeling.
It bars even the faintest perception
of pain and other signs of life.
It's a gas, isn't it?
How this "truth serum"
we call anesthesia
turns us inside out?
It loosens the hinges
of mind
and tongue.

No! Hear me out, doctor!
"You and your team are doing a great service."
I want you to know how great are these gifts
of skill, time, energy, and love
freely given to me
and the many who could,
or would not otherwise afford—
or perhaps risk—
this transfiguring opportunity.

Tonight, at the jazz and poetry event,
seated this time,
in another sort of theater,
I hear you giving voice
to gratitude.
It runs through your work;
it is echoed in the poems of your colleagues.

This gratitude is a lubricant.
It opens the heart and bows the head in easy reverence.
It draws together the palms
of even the self-proclaimed godless.
Around the world, it allows stiff knees to bend,
softening arms to reach out.

Like poems, and the act of creating them,
gratitude greases the wheel.
It adorns what for some,
amounts to merely going through the motions.

Gratitude is the gift that is given.
It is its own reward.
It is that which distinguishes good men,
and links the community of great souls.

God's Birthday

Remember who You are,
O Kalahansa—
"Eternal Swan",
child of God
found of Perfect Parentage.

O, Song of Siddha Masters,
send your sweet Voice
into vessels muted,
yearning for the Sound.

For God is Real
and all around,
your Destiny profound,
revealed,
abounds.

O, Immortal Swan,
on worldly waters
floating free,
in rippling waves
Divine.

All Saints attend
your day of birth—
their chorus
heard in heaven,
resounds
on earth.

Bruce
(Song)

You came to me with the dawn,
and you've stayed here all day long,
your warming presence in my heart, so good to me.
Though for years, I've been away,
I want to thank you for this day.
Because of you,
I know what true friends oughta be.

Refrain:
Best friend, know now, that I love you.
Best friend, it's right now that I care.
And in a quiet hour,
let this song become the flower,
bloomin' in your heart,
so you know I'm always there.

On the outside, I was bold,
but within the wind blew cold.
A woman-child, a life shaped by treachery.
I came to trust your special touch;
more than a word would've been too much.
You brought me to my Self,
and then stayed there with me.

(Refrain)

Today, you came again.
Door was open, you walked right in.
So glad that you could stay a little while.
Now, I hope before you're gone,
to give it back to you in song.
To keep you around this way just makes me smile.

(Refrain)

Friend

Nishanta:
seeing into silence:
the space between the breaths,
'tween dark and dawn,
the stillness in a bubbling stream,
the movement in soundless forest thickets.
Hear my heart-nest song:
love,
and blessed gratitude,
for bringing me along.

The Gift of Presence
(For Lois and Pinky)

Thank you.
for the gift:
your presence.
Life so simple
in its essence.

How could we know
that here,
we'd find
within our midst,
such hearts
so kind,

and open...
at this precious hour?
From your courage,
comes this flower
to greet each day
as it reveals:
the love that's shared,
is love
that heals.

7. Sing Peace Pilgrimage for Peace & Global Harmony

Peace Pilgrimage

"You will live in other people's houses,
and the work you do will be known
long after your name is forgotten."

This message, sung to me three times,
awakens me from my dream:
to listen, and write out the words and melody.
Their meaning, not yet apparent,
I take them into my *hatha yoga*
and meditation practice.

Opening the whirling, vertical vortex
to a cherished vision:
the flow and flowering
of a lifelong passion
to live by and to spread the message of peace—
peace within, peace among, peace with God.

You and I, friend;
you and I, troubadours—
journeying, making music together with others,
as living symbols of the peace we long to see
in this world.

Walking, riding, living in harmony with nature,
taking rest in homes, wherever we are welcomed
around the globe—
giving our hearts, minds and bodies
to the One, immutable and most loving Truth.

My Song
(Song)

Refrain:
And it's my song you hear me singing,
the one I've been living all along.
Its sweetness and its pain,
we've shared time and again.
And that's my song.
Yes, that's my song.

Singing your songs brings me pleasure,
as great as any I've known.
It's brought us closer together,
brought me comfort when I'm all alone.

Now a voice or voices inside me
are whispering and moving about.
And I hear and know what they're saying.
There's something inside trying to get out.

(Refrain)

Singing the songs that you gave me
always eased my troubles for awhile.
The promise that there's more where that came from
and meeting you this way makes me smile.

Though we never have stood face to face, friend,
and our paths have crossed only in song,
in the giving, I know I'm receiving.
It seems we've been friends all along.

(Refrain)

Misty Mountain Quest

In this Misty Mountain home,
earth, tree, water, stone
sound in me an ancient tone,
finding my comfort zone.

Rainforest mystery
'mid giant majesty,
soft-draped moss-strewn tapestry,
finding their weave in me.

While I in my hammock lay,
bubbling river songs relay,
dip naked: cool water, root, limb and clay
finding among them new ways to play.

In the misty morning air,
kingfisher, eagle songs we share,
touch each stone and place with care,
finding "stone family," I weep there.

Spot a lichen-coated driftwood shaft,
with saw and knife blade, a calming craft,
"Hoh H2O," my rain stick staff,
finding a friend to foot the path.

On a Misty Mountain Quest
exploring my comfort zone,
apart from the rest.
Winding upriver, silt-lined glacial pool, a test,
finding my dance, in pure waters, I'm blessed.

In a circle of sharing we are all bound
to share our quest,
hidden secrets we've found.
Pulling food from our packs, we offer 'round,
finding tribe among humans on this sacred ground.

In these encounters, I ask the earth to "teach me."
Listening to understand with honor, humor, humility.
Heart open in a land unbranded by human greed,
finding my home amid nature's ecstasy.

Earth Riddle Song

(Song, taken from the words of William McDonough)

What makes oxygen, fixes nitrogen,
sequesters carbon, distills water,
accrues solar energy as fuel,
makes complex sugars and food?
Creates microclimates?
Is self-replicating?
Changes colors with the seasons?
Oh, it's an ancient mystery,
this biodiversity,
microbial community and nature's university,
rainforest canopy,
shelter for you and me.
Tell me, is there anything so fine a design?
Is there anything so elegant, timeless, and relevant,
as a _____?

'Cause, what makes oxygen, fixes nitrogen,
sequesters carbon, distills water,
accrues solar energy as fuel,
makes complex sugars and food?
Creates microclimates?
Is self-replicating?
Changes colors with the seasons?

Oh, it's an ancient mystery,
this biodiversity,
microbial community and nature's university,
rainforest canopy,
shelter for you and me.
Tell me, is there anything so fine a design?
Is there anything so elegant, timeless and relevant,
as a tree?

So, for the love of all children for all time, everywhere.
For the love of all children for all time,
if we care.
For the love all children for all time;
for the love of all children, yours and mine;
for the love of all children,
of every kind:
save the trees.
Save the trees!
Save the trees!

Golden Token
(Song)

Like flickering stars
moved by the wind,
clouds of sea birds swoop and soar.
Not one falls that is not known.
A golden token calls him home,
where the red-gold horizon meets the shore.

We are bound for MacNeil Island, Federal Pen on Puget Sound.
Boarding the boat at sunset, a pink glow all around.
We take up places at the stern, our little band of three,
to rock across the water, chanting merrily.
To rock across the water, chanting merrily.

Refrain:
Hare Rama ke Rama ke Rama Hare Hare
Hare Krishna he Krishna he Krishna Hare Hare
Hare Rama ke Rama ke Rama Hare Hare
Hare Krishna he Krishna he Krishna Hare Hare
Rama Krishna Hare Hare

The wise old captain steps up to a prisoner down below,
and though his wrists are manacled, a light about him shone.
The boy, he sees, has not a bad heart,
his mistake, a simple one.
He's forgotten who he is, and why it is he's come.
He's forgotten who he is, and why it is he's come.

The captain says: "Son, who are you,
and why do you come here?"
The prisoner, with cast-down eyes, does not appear to hear.
Then, a light of recognition, something in the captain's tone,
he'd lost his way, forgot himself, went far astray from home.
He'd lost his way, forgot himself, went far astray from home.

(Refrain)

Now, the captain reaches for his hand,
and tenderly placed there
a golden token on his palm, the symbol of his care.
"This cylinder of gold I leave as symbol of your task,
to find for you the answer to these questions that I ask.
To find for you the answer to these questions that I ask."

He tells him: "Son, it's up to you to undertake to know,
just who you are and why you've come,
and where you want to go."
The captain's hand closed briefly over the young man's fist.
"God speed, go well," it signaled upon the handcuffed wrist.
"God speed, go well," it signaled upon the handcuffed wrist.

And that was when the boy looked up
into the boatman's eyes,
to see the tender look of love, beneficent and wise.
The sound of voices chanting, the three still at the stern;
the song they sing, awakening a soul's journey of return.
The song they sing, awakening a soul's journey of return.

(Refrain)

They reach the shore, he disembarks,
climbs to the prison gate.
the grating clank of metal appears to seal his fate.
In the red glow of the sunset, the chanting voices sound.
He holds the golden token, and his freedom, newly found.
He holds the golden token, and his freedom, newly found.

(Refrain 2x)

Circle of Seven Love Poems
(Song)

At what precious moment did I know
that if I spoke, you would hear me?
Your subtle presence awakens me at any hour,
demanding that I yield to you in love.

What is this rudeness of yours?
What is this ruthless love?
I've scarcely had a full night's rest,
Since my promise to do any damn fool thing
to keep this love alive within me.

I locked the door to my heart at nine last night.
At eleven, you stormed in,
waking me from a sound sleep,
and demanding I remember my promise to you.
Where did you get the key?

We were together all last night,
you in your bed, I in mine.
We spoke to each other
from some undetermined distance.
If this is a lie, then why
did you place your hands upon my shoulders,
and kiss the top of my head?
The cherries I'd saved for you
told you I knew.
"Om Namah Shivaya," you said.

Tell me.
What happened in your bed last night,
that softens your face
and sweetens your voice so?
The secret light in your eyes
is not concealed from love's gaze.

Tell me, you are not helpless!
Tell me, "I want none of your love!"
When the mother senses her child's hunger,
the breasts let down,
the milk flows.
Oh, beggar, don't be so proud!

Now, I come to you naked,
while you are still wearing your clothes.
I want to be embarrassed,
but my hand hides a grin.
Your eyes tease my heart as you pass by.
You know…

You Look Up!!

(Song)

The new dawn breaks, a fire-red ball,
off in the east, a silent call,

Refrain:
And you look up, up.
You look up!

The sight of wings against the sky,
an eagle soars, flyin' high.

(Refrain)

Now, when we swell with pride,
look down our nose,
or shuffle our feet,
look down at our toes,
when you forget it's all about love,
that's when life knocks you on your back
so you look up!

(Refrain)

A lightnin' flash, the thunder rolls,
a cooling breeze before the storm.

The summer rains on hot, dry ground,
reach out your hand when you hear the sound.

(Refrain)

But when your heart fills up with greed,
stuff danglin' off you, you don't even need,
if you grasp for more to fill your cup,
that's when life knocks you on your back
so you look up!

(Refrain)

The rain clouds part, the sun shines through,
and overhead, a rainbow's hues.

(Refrain)

The crescent moon is on the rise.
The nighttime stars light up the skies.
And you look up, up,
you look up!

8. Saving the Best
for Last

After All

Who, or what, after all,
remains after initiation?
The in-dwelling Lord,
having been away
on his worldly sojourn
reclaims His throne,
making His presence known
to the bound soul.

Everything that takes place from then on
is for the sake of *sadhana*.

Agocharam

(Chant heard in a dream)

Agocharam tu baahayatah.
Agocharam tu baahayatah.

Tam tam agocharam.
Agocharam tam agocharam.

I see the one who is otherwise beyond perception:
"That." That is beyond perception.

Afterword

A seed of love planted at conception bursts forth with undeniable power as the soul exits the womb into the light of day. Love made manifest in human form is God's work. The journey undertaken, however short or long, through however many vehicles and lifetimes, is most simply the recognition and acknowledgment of Love as the medium, substance and course the seed is meant to embody and experience.

A mere droplet in the endless, all-pervasive ocean of Consciousness is charged with a great mission: to emerge on the world stage only to become reabsorbed in the sweet nectar that spawned it - Divine Love.

It has been said that every such noble work is, at first, impossible. Yet, the deck is stacked favorably for the seed, this tiny droplet, in that its very nature is of the earth and ocean, the Divine stuff of which it is made. It will be apparent, therefore, when it arrives home aga▮

We are never alone. Even when the reflection of our true mission is a bit smudged and distorted, help is as near as the breath.

"Help!"

Help, the great mantra of the most dense, pissed off, proud and resistant, is nearest at hand when the light inside goes on. "Ask and you shall receive," is so for every living soul. The answer is there, though too often rejected and neglected.

The toddler says, "I do it myself!" The nineteen-year-old knows it all.

And the thirty-two year old will likely say (or think), "You can't tell me what to do!"

But the dialogue with the Divine begins and is sustained by a listening ear and a willing heart. What is heard and heeded resonates like one's own song. It draws to itself sincere and enlightened helpers in human form who have set out ahead and can shine a light on the road less-traveled.

I have met so many since that one desperate cry for help at age 39. As precious benefactors, their function, to the extent that they were able and that I was open to receiving, has been to offer encouragement, provide insight and facilitate growth in awareness.

My poems, songs and visions exemplify my having circled, time and again, over the same territory. Hence, I, myself, have been able to act as road-worker, pointing to signs for other seekers. As in the game of Monopoly, "Do not pass Go, do not collect $200." In other words, there may be a simpler, more direct and harmonious way to arrive at one's destination.

The question, then, is "Where are you going?"

My search was underway, but I didn't really know where it was leading. I'd despaired of ever meeting a guide that I could trust to show me the goal and how to get there. The miracle is that I experienced both in my spiritual awakening. The challenge for me, then, became to sustain its realization.

Few, if any, have escaped this journey without missteps - wreaking havoc and violence or falling victim to it. The boomerang principle, "what goes around comes around," comes into play in everyone's quest.

Fear and self-loathing - ignorance - with an underlying sense of unworthiness and the impulse to do something to fix or succumb to it sets the scene for a battle between forces that can't be settled without full surrender to "what is."

I was surprised on meeting my guru for the first time to hear him say, "Let it go," in reply to someone who asked, "What can I do about the hate I feel toward my parents?"

It wasn't my question, but I couldn't get it out of my thoughts. For several days running, I felt the skin on my forearms, my reaching out muscles, peeling away. Neither of my parents knew nor would they approve of my whereabouts, but this subtle yet persistent feeling prompted me to write to each of them. I told them where I was and who I was with, imparting the guru's message to "See God in your Self and others."

The Self-respect I'd shown myself by letting go of self-directed hatred that had been turned outward was echoed in their heartfelt responses. Hostilities ceased, order was restored. The healing that was taking place within me clearly impacted generations extending back and forward in our family's lineage.

To imagine a transcendent, attainable godliness is almost heretical to street corner preachers and religious pundits. But within the folds of the highest teachings is the Truth, that the only use for the human body is the attainment of Love... Divine, Irrefutable Love. Here, now, while still in the body. Once established, the soul may move on to higher realms, or, in the case of a true master, may choose to walk the walk and talk the talk in the service of other seeds and droplets who happen to be inhabiting a body.

When desire in its many guises and permutations gives way to that one, inevitable fact of human birth, the Universe - Consciousness, God - has room to work.

The sage, Narada, in his sutras on Divine Love says that the nature of love is Amrita. A, meaning "not," and mrta, meaning "death." In other words, the ultimate destination of the soul is "immortality." The body may drop away from life to life, but the soul may never again reincarnate. The soul never dies.

Evelyn Underhill, in her book, Mysticism, expresses the journey in this way: "The spiritual pilgrim goes because s/he is called; because she wants to go, must go, if she is to find rest and peace. 'God needs man,' says [Meister] Eckhart. It is Love calling to love, and the journey, though in one sense a hard pilgrimage, up and out by the terraced mount and the ten heavens to God, in another is the inevitable rush of the roving comet, caught, at last, to the Central Sun."

I was on my way when the elixir of Divine Love entered and filled my body and awareness at my awakening. Nothing. No thing in my prior life experience of love could compare to this nectar. Its memory can and could be summoned in meditation and the other practices I was guided to as a pathway opened to me.

I am still on that path. There are many. I taught meditation to women who were abused by men and to men in a federal prison and state reformatory some of whom had hurt women. When one of the men queried whether the path that I followed was for him, I suggested he ask the question in a quiet moment within his own heart. His dilemma was resolved by the time we next met.

Growing up, religion was anathema to me. My friends could not talk to me about God. My Mother had been burned by the church because she loved to dance. In her eyes, religion was a "crutch" and the "opiate of the masses." But as my search for the nature of reality proceeded, I was attracted to and quite literally surrounded by a circle of friends who had met a Guru. I didn't understand why, though numerous signs of his presence in my life had been appearing. Our dialogue awaited my reply. Even while three thousand miles apart, there was no denying him with the "Coming of the Light."

May this offering of my poems, songs and visions serve as encouragement to seek and find the path and guide that resonate most vibrantly within your heart space where love and wisdom meet.

Glossary*

Arati – Waving of lights and chanting ceremony typically performed at dawn and dusk

Baba – Affectionate name bestowed upon a spiritual master

Brahman – Ultimate Reality, the ground of the Universe, the Absolute

Darshan – Seeing or being in the presence of an accomplished one, a guru.

Diwali – Indian New Year

Ganesha – elephant-headed God, the remover of obstacles

Guru – teacher, preceptor, the one who removes the darkness of ignoranc

Hare Rama, Hare Krishna – a chant honoring Lords Rama and Krishna, incarnations of the ultimate Reality

Meditation – mind flowing in an unbroken current toward a particular object

Nataraj – Lord of the Dance, *Shiva*, the cosmic play

Om Namah Shivaya – mantra, I honor the eternal Reality within me

Purno a'ham vimarsha – the perfect, "I" awareness

Sadhana – self-effort, spiritual discipline, the path, the means to liberatio

Satsang – the company of saints and devotees, the company of the good

Satchidananda – being, consciousness and bliss absolute

Shakti – the power, divine cosmic energy

Shiva – ultimate Reality, the Creator

Shiva lingam – a form of the formless

Shri Guru Gita – a garland of mantras in Sanskrit, honoring the spiritual teacher explicating the cosmic nature of the Guru and liberating role in the life of disciples

*Definitions borrowed from John Grimes' A Concise Dictionary of Indian Philosophy: Sanskrit Terms Defined in English

"Earth Riddle Song"—The song lyrics come, in part, from a Ted Talk given by William McDonough, an American architect, academic, and community designer. In describing his own book, Cradle to Cradle, McDonough says in his talk that the book is a polymer. And then he describes what goes into making a tree, which is what most books are printed on:

"...and to use something as elegant as a tree, imagine this design assessment: Design something that makes oxygen, sequesters carbon, fixes nitrogen, distills water, accrues solar energy as fuel, makes complex sugars and food, creates microclimates, changes colors with the seasons, and self-replicates. Well, why don't we knock that down and write on it?"

The link:
https://ted2sub.org/talks/william_mcdonough_cradle_to_cradle_design

"Agocharam tu baahayatah" is a Sanskrit phrase that the author heard in a dream. The translation was made with the help of Bhau Shastri Vaijapurkar.

About the Author: Pushkara Sally Ashford

Poems strewn throughout her journals and songs inspired by dreams and visions chronicle Pushkara's healing quest and spiritual journey.

The collection represents the search of a soul longing to experience and recognize in full awareness the purpose of a human birth. The sequence of chapters hints at the most secret and treasured of all journeys made over the course of a long life. It is a simple offering out of gratitude for the abundance of grace in coming to know where and how to look for answers, and for her heart space having been sufficiently open to receive them.

Joyful music-making among her family members offset the specter and tensions that were universally felt around the "war effort" in 1940. Nee, Sally Irene, she was born on the eve of WWII in Los Angeles. Her quest for a pathway to peace and global harmony is the thread that runs from beginning to end of her long life. It is aptly described in a childhood nursery rhyme: "With rings on her fingers and bells on her toes, she shall have music wherever she goes."

The family always made music. Her Dad played the saxophone. Grandma played a rollicking honky tonk piano. She learned from her Mother how to sing harmony. Her parents sang together in a chorus.

They were always on the move, her Dad following the work from California to Oregon and on to Idaho. During the years that her parents and grandparents traded off round-the-clock shifts at the shipyards in Vancouver, Washington, Pushkara and her two sisters stayed overnight and made mischief in a nearby barracks nursery school. They moved to Seattle in 1945. Soon after, Dad left work in the shipyards and partnered to form a construction company.

Pushkara sang harmony from a young age with her sister, Marj. In her teens, Pushkara, with her sister, her best friend, Kae, and her sister, ReeAnn, joined a folk chorus, The Wayfarers. At 18, she sang and led songs in a folk trio, The Cascades, and performed in a duo with her husband, John, at folk festivals, world fairs, in libraries, churches, longterm care facilities, at camps and conferences, in coffeehouses, on cruises, in schools and parks, on college campuses, radio and television. She performed on stage in plays, musicals and operas.

After birthing three children, the "activist gene" imparted to her by her Mom, a flaming radical, moved Pushkara to become an initiator and change agent, co-founder and creative designer of social, educational and community projects, programs and events. Pushkara was a co-founder of the Seattle Folklore Society and its Song Circle which met at the Clubhouse in the University District.

Seattle's first K-8 public alternative school began in collaboration with her neighbor. In 1970, they hosted 20 students in their homes for several months before a proposal set forth by the New School Movement was finally funded and assigned a building by the Seattle Public School District. Her sons, age 10 and 7 were enrolled. Pushkara was on hand when the school opened, first as a parent volunteer and later as a primary classroom teacher. Music could be heard in the halls where children of all ages gathered to sing together.

Keeping a home, having babies, music-making and performance had delayed Pushkara's undergraduate education which stretched over seventeen years and was finally capped in 1978 by a Masters Degree in Social Work. Professional opportunities came from every direction.

Pushkara was a Home and Family Life instructor for cooperative preschools in the Home and Family Life program at Seattle Community College. She also taught a course in music for children for preschool teachers in that program and was teaching a class in creative therapeutic modalities for masters in psychology students at Antioch University.

During the same period, Pushkara was hired to design and coordinate an innovative program that addressed family violence. In that role, she began a community awareness campaign and formed interdisciplinary teams, bringing together legal, law enforcement, medical personnel, therapeutic and addiction services, advocacy and shelters for women in abusive relationships. Her caseload included individual and couples therapy. She led groups for women who had been abused as children, as well as, for teen girls whose lives were currently impacted by violence in their homes.

In private practice, Pushkara offered a stress reduction workshop she'd developed: "A Repertoire for Self-Care," which she was invited to Minneapolis to conduct for Montessori teachers. She was leading a song at a gathering with friends when she noted a bewildering change. As a singer, she knew her voice. She'd been leading workshops, "In Search of a Voice," for adults who believed they could not sing. At first, though only the slightest interruption - that is, silence where the sound would ordinarily be sustained, this moment signaled an intractable condition that soon led to a medical diagnosis of spasmodic dysphonia. Other than the obvious stress of a hectic, outwardly directed life, its roots were left to Pushkara to discover.

Divine intervention in a life is often misunderstood and rarely welcomed. So while she struggled to recoup and maintain the momentum of her family and professional life through an increasingly fragile illusion of health, her present circumstances were leading Pushkara inward, toward her own soul. It was time. A profound spiritual awakening and subsequent near-death experience provide context for Pushkara's healing quest that brought a spiritual master and teacher of meditation into her life and took her around the world to places and people she would not otherwise have encountered. This is the journey recounted in her journals and in the poems, songs and visions published for the first time in "Breathing Life into Death."

Pushkara lays no claim to fame as a poet or songwriter, yet both songs and poems emerged from within only after she lost the mellifluous singing voice she'd once been known for. Her journey has been in the being and living through experience with a fervent prayer for resonance and connection in sharing some part of it with others.

The singing dream she woke with in 2008 brought visions to mind of a gypsy wagon journey, SingPeace! Pilgrimage for Peace and Global Harmony. It has returned Pushkara to her first love of singing and making music. She designed and commissioned the construction of the wagon in 2009 and gathered troubadours together to go on the road. Their voices joining with communities in multi-layered harmonies are the outward expression and reflection of a culture of peace, the practice that Pushkara continues to envision and uphold within her heart. Readers are invited to learn more about SingPeace! online where they can interact and share their responses and experiences.

https://singpeacepilgrimage.ning.com/home

www.ingramcontent.com/pod-product-compliance
Lightning Source LLC
Chambersburg PA
CBHW021646120626
46545CB00002B/728